TV's Fabulous Faces

by PEGGY HERZ

Scholastic Book Services
New York Toronto London Auckland Sydney Tokyo

Published by Scholastic Book Services, a division of Scholastic Magazines, Inc.

12 11 10 9 8 7 6 5 4 7 8 9/7 0 1 2/8

Printed in the U.S.A.

03

Contents

Laverne and Shirley (Penny Marshall, right, and Cindy Williams, left) were so popular on *Happy Days*, that ABC decided to give them a series of their own. And *Laverne and Shirley* is a big hit!

Laverne and Shirley:
Doin' It *Their* Way

Laverne and Shirley came on the air in January, 1976, and surprised everybody by zooming right to the top of the ratings! Overnight, the show became the biggest new comedy hit of the season. The reason? It's different. Refreshingly different.

Laverne and Shirley are fun-loving and fast-talking. They aren't glamorous secretaries or sophisticated TV producers. In fact, they aren't like anybody else on TV. They work in the bottle-cap division of a beer company. They punch a time clock, do their work, go bowling, eat pizza, and dream about the future.

They don't live in a beautiful apartment with a maid and a doorman. They live in a basement apartment in Milwaukee. The men who live upstairs aren't tall, dark, and handsome. They are Lenny and Squiggy — and Prince Charmings they *aren't!* You need earplugs when Lenny and Squiggy are around, in fact, which is most of the time.

Laverne and Shirley struggled through high school together and now they're struggling to make it out in the "real world." It isn't always easy, even with Carmine, Lenny, and Squiggy to help them.

Producer Garry Marshall came up with the idea for *Laverne and Shirley*. At first, the two girls were to be in one episode of *Happy Days* and that was all. Garry decided to keep it "all in the family"; he called his sister Penny.

"He asked me if I was doing anything that week," Penny recalled with a smile. "I said no, so he asked me if I wanted to play a role on *Happy Days*. I said sure. Then he asked Cindy Williams to play Shirley and she agreed. We did the show and had a good time."

But that wasn't the end of Laverne and Shirley. Viewers liked the two zany characters and said so. Three weeks later, Garry Marshall proposed a *Laverne and Shirley* series to ABC. The network liked the idea.

"It all happened very quickly," Penny said. "We had to do the first shows very fast. When we looked at them later, we saw that there had been too much yelling. We've toned down the series since then. There isn't as much yelling."

Penny is married to actor Rob Reiner. Rob plays

Capping bottles at the Shotz Brewery may not be a glamorous job—but for Laverne DeFazio it's a way to earn a living!

Mike Stivic, Archie Bu *Family*. "Rob and I und "He knows the press series."

Penny add
neighborh
we'd mee
of schoo [redacted]

Penny grew up in New York City. "In the Bronx," she said. Her father was a film-maker and her mother was a dancing teacher.

Having a mother who ran a dancing school meant that Penny took a lot of dancing lessons, whether she wanted to or not. "Every year I threatened to quit," Penny admitted. "My mother would say, 'Okay, you do the grocery shopping and the cleaning like all the other kids do on Saturday.' " Penny smiled. "I didn't know anybody who did that, but the threat kept me in dancing school. Whenever one of my dates came to the door to pick me up, my mother would ask him, 'Do you dance? Sing? Will you pull curtains for the show?' "

Penny always loved going to camp. "I went every summer from the time I was eight," she said.

"I loved junior high school. But I didn't like high school. It was an all-girls school."

Penny was put in an honors class during her sophomore year in high school. "I had a high IQ, but I was not a good worker. I tried to get out of the honors class. I wanted to be like everybody else," she said.

"School wasn't the center of activity, anyway,"
[redacted]ded. "The neighborhood was. Kids in the
[redacted]ood went to all different schools. Then
[redacted] on the fence after school. I didn't join a lot
[redacted] activities, but I hung out on the fence a lot. I didn't want to miss anything! From there you could see what was going on down on the parkway, you could see what was going on in the candy store, and so on. Then on Friday nights we'd all go to the movies in a group.

"Boys were my only great interest at any time. Acting didn't come until I had dropped out of college. In junior high I was in a play only because it could get me out of science and math. I was very embarrassed when I did it, though."

Laverne and Shirley confer in their apartment before going out on dates.

Penny had many friends in school. "I was always joking around," she remembered. "The guys I liked didn't necessarily like me on a dating basis, but we were friends. I was not an attractive child — and I was a tomboy on top of it."

Penny went to college at the University of New Mexico, which is a long way from the Bronx. "I wanted to go to Ohio State," she said, "but New Mexico was eager for out-of-state students. My mother wasn't too good at geography. She thought New Mexico was closer to New York than Ohio! She also liked it because it had a new infirmary and a new cafeteria. Those were her main requirements: Eat and be well."

Penny married a football player and dropped out of college during her junior year. "One of us had to go to work," she explained. At first, she worked as a secretary. Then, after her daughter was born, Penny decided to teach dancing. "I needed something physical to do," she said. "I had gained a lot of weight." So all her dancing lessons paid off, after all. Eventually, they led her into acting.

A little theater group in town asked her to direct the dances in a show. She said no, but agreed to be in the chorus. She did well, and friends began to encourage her to take up acting.

One thing about acting really appealed to her. "They stay up late at night!" she laughed. "I like

"Help!" yells Shirley, surrounded by a swarm of bottles. Will they ever stop coming?

that! I come alive at 4:30 in the afternoon. I like to stay up until about 3:00 a.m.!"

She began to get speaking parts in plays. Her first marriage ended in divorce, but her acting career was just beginning. "I decided I wanted to get out of Albuquerque," she said. "I had two choices. I could either go back to New York to my parents, or I could go to California where my brother Garry was."

She decided on California. In the summer of 1967, she left New Mexico and headed for Los Angeles with her baby girl. At first, things weren't easy. She took temporary jobs. But she stuck it out. And, finally, acting parts began to come along. Penny played

Jack Klugman's secretary in *The Odd Couple* and has had roles in other TV series, including the role of a nurse named Paula on *The Mary Tyler Moore Show*. But nothing captured the hearts of TV viewers like her playing of Laverne De Fazio.

* * *

Laverne is a realist. "This is it. This is our life," is her attitude. Her friend, Shirley Feeney, is a dreamer. She's waiting for the man of her dreams to drive up in a sleek car and wisk her away. But it looks as if only Lenny and Squiggy are available at the moment, so Shirley is still waiting.

Cindy Williams, who plays Shirley Feeney, wasn't really sure she wanted to be in a TV series. She'd been doing movies and stage plays. "I wasn't sure I wanted to lock myself into playing the same character every week," Cindy told me. "I didn't want to be typecast. I no longer worry about that, though. I understand now how many characters I can play. Shirley is a part of me, but I'm not playing myself. She is a character I play.

"I'm not going to have the powerful impact of a character like Fonzie," Cindy added. "I have a changeable face. I photograph differently if my hair is long or if it's short or whatever. I can look totally different. I was concerned about that at first but now I think I'm lucky. It makes it easier for me to play many different roles."

Cindy was born in Van Nuys, California. "I was 16 when I decided I wanted to be an actress," she said. "Before that I wanted to be a nurse. The drama of it appealed to me — and the costume. I could see myself throwing open the door of the operating room and crying, 'Stand back! Plasma arriving!' "

Cindy liked school. "I didn't get good grades, though," she said. "I just couldn't concentrate. I'd be off daydreaming or making jokes in my head. I'd look around at the other kids and wonder about them. I was interested in people."

Cindy laughed. "One day when we were having an algebra test, the teacher had the shortest boy in class pass out the test papers with the tallest boy. I went through the entire test wondering why he had done that. The two boys looked ridiculous together. I flunked the test.

"My parents wanted me to learn a good, decent trade. I learned to type 30 words a minute — with 19 errors. I tried to explain that I was double jointed and couldn't get the right pressure on the keys."

High school was the best time of her life, Cindy said. "I was into and out of everything," she explained. "But gradually I began to get more and more involved in drama."

After high school graduation, Cindy went to Los Angeles City College. "I was totally wrapped up in theater arts by then," she said. "Mainly I wanted to get up and act! I was very nervous in college. I knew the next step was LIFE."

She delayed taking that step as long as possible. For several years after she graduated from college, she didn't do any acting. "But then I realized that was wrong," she admitted, "and I started up again."

After minor roles in several films and TV shows, she was chosen for a role in George Cukor's film, *Travels With My Aunt*. Then she was cast in *American Graffiti*, playing Ron Howard's girl friend, and in *The Conversation*. She had met Garry Marshall early in her career — and he remembered her when he needed someone to play Shirley Feeney.

I met Cindy one afternoon after *Laverne and Shirley* had been in rehearsal all day. "It's been a long day," she admitted. "We've been on our feet all day, with only five-minute breaks here and there. It's like being a waitress, only you don't get any tips!"

Cindy is single and lives in Beverly Hills. "I'll go home now and do nothing," she said.

"Are you a good cook?" I asked her.

"Last night I cooked a good meal," she answered. "But I don't do that very often. I usually have a cup of soup — and Oreo cookies about 2:00 a.m."

Cindy and Henry Winkler, who plays Fonzie on *Happy Days*, have been friends for a long time. "He's an old buddy," she said. She has no special

Laverne and Shirley are true friends till the end. This zany pair have won the hearts and tickled the funnybones of millions of TV viewers.

boyfriend at the moment. "I have one Siamese cat," she explained, "and I love to play backgammon and cards.

"I hope I won't be changed by the success of *Laverne and Shirley*," Cindy added. "I don't think I will. It's a joy to be recognized by so many people. I sometimes feel very humbled by it."

Arm in arm, Laverne and Shirley have sung, danced, and laughed their way into the hearts of millions of TV viewers. They are making their dreams come true. And they are sharing the fun with all of us.

The Robot Cop: John Schuck in **Holmes and Yoyo**

"John Schuck plays a *what?*" I asked.

"A robot policeman in *Holmes and Yoyo,*" answered the ABC spokesman.

Well, I thought, I guess that's one way to outdo Kojak and Columbo. After all, *they* are mere human beings!

"Would you like to interview him?" I was asked.

"A robot?" I asked doubtfully. "What's he like?"

"He's very nice."

How could I resist? I've interviewed Kojak and Columbo — why not a robot named Yoyo? Real robots are machines that look like human beings. John Schuck is a human being playing a machine — and that's a real switch!

John also happens to be Sgt. Charles Enright in NBC's *McMillan and Wife* — so I had no trouble recognizing him when he walked into our interview. He wasn't even wired up to his computer, in fact!

Yoyo, I learned, is a robot with an electronic, computerized system. It is a very advanced system, but sometimes things go wrong, causing all kinds of problems for Yoyo and his partner, Holmes (who is not a robot).

"Yoyo behaves like a human being," John explained. "He doesn't behave like a machine in a mechanical way. He's been programmed to be good at one thing — and that's police detective work. He has no amazing physical abilities. He's not a man of tremendous strength. He's not superior in that way. He has a photographic memory, speaks many languages, and he can do imitations very well. He can be hurt as any machine can be hurt — he can be broken.

"Monsters have always been popular in literature and in humor," John pointed out. "That's basically what Yoyo is. We love machines and gadgets. We love dolls we can take apart and put back together."

John loves playing roles in two different TV series, he said. He's a policeman in both — but there's quite a difference between the two!

John has been acting for some time. "I was born in Boston, but I spent most of my young life in Buffalo, New York," he said. "My father was an English professor at Buffalo State."

At one point, the family lived in New Jersey, not far from New York City. "We had an album of the musical *Oklahoma,*" John recalled. "I loved it. I used to sing along with it. On my fifth birthday, my parents took me into New York to see *Oklahoma* on the stage. We sat in the front row and I sang along there too. It was wonderful. I think I've probably

Which button to press? Holmes (Richard B. Shull) tries to figure out the computer mysteries of his robot partner Yoyo (John Schuck).

wanted to be an actor from then on. I loved the theater so much. I was in many of the school plays."

After high school, John enrolled at Denison University in Granville, Ohio. He graduated with majors in theater, philosophy, and English. "We had our own summer theater there," John said. "In 11 weeks we put on 10 plays. *Oklahoma* was the first musical I did in college," he laughed. He hadn't even forgotten the words, he discovered!

John was appearing at a theater in in San Francisco when movie producer Robert Altman came to a performance. "We took an instant dislike to each

Yoyo is a robot of many parts—he can catch a criminal, memorize important police information, speak many languages—even brew a great cup of coffee!

other," John recalled. "He thought my acting was arrogant — and it was. I thought he was weird. We talked some. Five weeks later he called and offered me the role of the dentist in the movie *M*A*S*H*. That film changed so many lives, including mine.

"I'm a great believer that things happen to you if you're open," John continued. "Everything that has happened to me has seemed so natural. You just have to prepare yourself so you'll be ready for whatever happens to you. I consider myself very lucky to be working. There is so little employment for actors!"

John has one bit of advice for young people. "Learn to say 'yes' to yourself," he said. "We all fail. We all hurt at times. You have to learn to go through those times and then say to yourself, 'Well, I've been through that. Now I'm ready to go on.'

"I went through a difficult period when I was in junior and senior high school," he said. "My family was helpful, but I felt a communications gap. I was painfully shy. I didn't date much until college. Things didn't work out for me. I was a good ballroom dancer. Then Chubby Checker came along and everyone was doing the twist!"

One thing John Schuck isn't, and that's a robot! He bubbles over with enthusiasm and enjoyment, in fact!

"I find great joy in everything I do," he explained.

"I love to laugh — and I'm getting good at laughing at myself. I love sailing. I play a little tennis. And I read everything."

In two series, John is doing his best to make people laugh and enjoy themselves. It takes talent to do that — human talent, that is. There are some things computers just can't do!

Even a complex machine like Yoyo can get rusty. Then it's up to partner Holmes to get him back in order!

Gabe Kotter and His Sweathogs:
Welcome Back, Kotter

Who would have believed that a TV series about a group of students called the "Sweathogs" would become one of the top shows on the air? That's exactly what happened to *Welcome Back, Kotter*, a comedy series about a Brooklyn high school teacher and his class of "underachievers."

Comedian Gabriel Kaplan plays Gabe Kotter, the teacher.* Why is the name of the show *Welcome Back, Kotter*? Because Kotter was once a student at James Buchanan High School in Brooklyn — the school setting for the TV series. Kotter was one of the losers. Then he decided to go to college and become a teacher. Now he's back there, teaching a class of students with "special problems."

"The kids are troublemakers, but in a harmless way," John Travolta told me in an interview. John plays Vinnie Barbarino, one of the ringleaders in

Kotter's class. "They give the teacher a hard time," John added. "But that's part of being in school! There's never been a series on TV about a class like this. Kids are getting a bigger kick out of the show than anyone else."

Gabe Kaplan helped create the series. He based the characters on people he knew when he was in high school — in Brooklyn, New York, of course! He worked hard to get into the show the types of people he remembered, including the wheeler-dealer, the yo-yo, the clown, and so on.

Gabe Kaplan actually attended a high school in Brooklyn. Erasmus Hall was a school very much like James Buchanan in the TV series, and although Kaplan wasn't exactly a loser, he didn't make it all the way through to graduation.

"I left my senior year," he said during a luncheon interview. "I have some happy memories of school, but mainly it was a pretty confusing time. I didn't know what I wanted to do. I had decided I was not going to college. I saw nothing I wanted that I could get with a high school diploma. I was missing some credits, so I wouldn't have graduated that year, anyway. What I really wanted to do was play baseball."

Students in Gabe's high school were rated in a one-through-five system. "I was always in the fours," Gabe recalled. "That was next to the dumbest. Once you tell a kid that, he stops trying.

"I was 17 when I left school. I was a good baseball player, but not great. I tried out for minor league clubs in Florida and Texas. You didn't need that much money to try out. I had some savings and I took odd jobs to make money."

He didn't make it as a baseball player, though. "For four years I did various things — mainly nothing," he admitted.

Gabe didn't have any teachers like Mr. Kotter, or things might have been different. "I was turned off by school," he said. "Nobody in school showed any interest in me. Sometimes they would call me in and say I did well on tests, why wasn't my average higher? Everything they said was fine, then I'd leave the room and that would be it. I never had a Mr. Kotter or anybody like him.

"I was really drifting during those years after I left school. I made money and spent it. I was really lucky. Anything could have happened to me. At that point, my chances of being happy and successful were very slim. I don't recommend what I did," Gabe stressed. "It's better to stay in school."

One summer Gabe took a job as a bellboy at a Lakewood, New Jersey, hotel. He spent his free time watching stand-up comics do their routines. And suddenly one day he said to himself: "Hey, I can do that!"

He was 21 when he began his new career. "In the

Comedian Gabe Kaplan plays Gabe Kotter, the Sweathogs' favorite teacher. He helped to create the *Welcome Back, Kotter* series, basing the characters on people he knew when he was a high school student in Brooklyn, New York.

beginning I did jokes and things I had heard older comics do," Gabe said. "I wasn't doing anything very original." Slowly he began to develop his own material and style. "I began to talk about my personal life," he told me. His comedy act began to take off. He started to play the better clubs and to appear on various TV talk shows and specials. He'd found the secret. "Now I don't do anything that doesn't come from my own personal feelings," he said.

One night in August, 1974, he was appearing at The Comedy Store in West Hollywood when producer Alan Sacks dropped by. Sacks was also born in Brooklyn and Gabe's routine about his Brooklyn school days cracked him up. Shortly afterward, Sacks and Gabe Kaplan got together over lunch — and the idea for the *Welcome Back, Kotter* series was born. They took their idea to executive producer James Komack, a former stand-up comedian himself. At first, Komack didn't like the idea. But he came around, and sold ABC on the idea of a series. Then the problems *really* began.

Casting was one of the problems. Could Hollywood actors play Brooklyn high school students? Gabe didn't think so. He wanted them to go to New York and interview actors there. He finally got his way. "We narrowed the field down from 200," Gabe recalled. "We picked the best. All had had New York experience; all were experienced actors."

Concerned teacher Gabe Kotter is constantly clashing with harried assistant principal, Mr. Woodman (John Sylvester White).

The producers put together a *Welcome Back, Kotter* film which ABC showed to its affiliated stations. Many of the station managers didn't like it. They thought the kids were "too threatening."

"Kids liked it, but many adults didn't like the first show," Gabe admitted.

As the weeks went by, however, more and more viewers began to take to the show. And Gabe and his Sweathogs learned from each other. "I wasn't an actor," Gabe said. "I watched them and learned. And they learned from me — about timing and working before an audience. Each of the four young actors had to develop his own character. They've all done that."

The success of the series has sent Gabe's career into orbit. He is in great demand for personal appearances around the country. "Some people come to see me as Mr. Kotter," Gabe said with a smile. "Others come to see Gabe Kaplan, the comedian. So I talk about the show, how it began, and so on.

"The characters in the show are universal," Gabe added. "Everybody knows a Horshack, a Barbarino...they're very appealing. Mr. Kotter is the teacher everyone would like to have. He treats kids as individuals and as human beings."

Ron Palillo as Horshack:
"Oh, Oh...Mr. Kotter! Mr. Kotter!"

Ron Palillo and I had lunch one day in the cafeteria at ABC. *Welcome Back, Kotter* was in rehearsal that day. Cast members were eating at various tables around the dining room and Gabe Kaplan was sitting nearby, throwing jokes in our direction. The *Kotter* group has become a close-knit family. They like and respect each other.

I asked Ron how the series had changed his life.

"It hasn't changed it in outward ways," he replied. "It's just nice to have some security. It's nicer to know I have some money stashed away so I can get through the tough times if they happen. Also, I suppose it's changed my life because now people know who I am. And they are a lot nicer to me!"

"Mention the star of the show!" Gabe called over.

Ron just grinned and continued. "I like to lead a quiet life. I like privacy," he said. "In that respect my life has not changed."

Ron was doing a play in New York City when he got the part of Horshack. He didn't really want to try

Horshack (Ron Palillo) lets it all hang out as Barbarino (John Travolta) looks on. Ron thinks that *Kotter* touches on some real problems of kids in school today.

out for a part in the *Kotter* series, but his agent thought he should. "I knew the character was supposed to be someone tough. I tried to dress so I looked tough. When I walked in, Gabe and Alan Sacks took one look at me and said, "If you can act, you've got the part." Ron laughed. "Then they found out I wasn't really tough."

Horshack has a very unusual voice and laugh. Ron said that happened by accident. "My voice came out that way in the first reading," he said. "It probably happened because I was nervous. I knew I was supposed to use a Brooklyn accent—it came out kind of a cross between a whine and a groan.

"At first," Ron explained, "Horshack was supposed to be the class loser. But as we did the shows, it came out that Horshack is probably the smartest one in the class. He is really opening up now.

"I didn't want Horshack to be a cartoon character who laughed at everything," Ron said. "Horshack had been acting dumb for a reason. He started out as a kind of mascot for the other kids. Now he's one of them. He's becoming more and more himself. That's what Kotter has done for him. All of the kids are changing for the better because of this teacher. If Kotter weren't there, Horshack probably would never have learned."

When the show first came on the air, some viewers thought Horshack was retarded. "That made me very angry,'' Ron said. ''People pinned that label on Horshack because he is young. If you act that way when you're older, they just say you're a little slow.''

Ron shook his head in disgust. ''At first, Horshack would talk only when Barbarino said, 'You may talk now.' That's going on in schools today. It always has! Retarded? Go to schools and see the kids! Many of them are crying out for attention and that's not because they are retarded! They are asking for help!

''Horshack is doing the same thing. He has no family life. His only life is Gabe Kotter and the other kids. His family life is terrible!'' Ron smiled. ''He'll always be a little weird, of course, because Horshack *is* weird. But he's not afraid any more to show that he's smart. He's not afraid to disagree with his friends.''

Just then, Gabe Kaplan finished his lunch and walked by. ''Just say the star is the best,'' he joked, and Ron laughed.

''I think the show is popular, not because it's set in Brooklyn, but because we touch on things that really happen,'' Ron noted. ''It doesn't matter where you come from. Everybody has known someone like these characters. I also think we're touching on real issues and real problems. In the show we're working on right now the guys are forming a gang and Horshack wants no part of it. That's peer pressure. A lot of our shows deal with peer pressure.''

Ron was born in New Haven, Connecticut. His father was the Postmaster of Whitneyville, Connecticut. "My father died when I was nine," Ron said. "Shortly after that, the Cheshire Community Theatre was doing a play. My mother thought it would be good for me to get out and meet people. I got a part in the play — and for a long time she was sorry she encouraged me! I got hooked on it and she was afraid I'd end up being an actor with no money."

Theater became his greatest interest. When he was 14, he started his own theater and ran it for four years. It was called the Black Friars Summer Theatre, and it was a successful venture.

Ron graduated from the University of Connecticut with a Bachelor of Fine Arts degree in theater. "My mother worked at four or five jobs to put my brothers and sister through college," he said. "I got a scholarship and worked summers."

After graduation, Ron toured with a Shakespeare company and appeared with a repertory company in Florida. "That experience was invaluable," he pointed out. "It has helped me a great deal in doing this series.

"I'm an actor," he added. "I've played many roles. Horshack is an important part of my life but I'm not him." He paused and smiled. "I had two or three friends in high school," he said. "I was Horshack then in a sense. I was a strange kid. I was kind of a weirdo in high school myself. But Horshack went out and looked for friends his own age and got them. I found I could relate better to older people. At 14 and 15 I was hanging around with college kids. My father's death made me grow up fast."

When he's not working, Ron enjoys running and swimming. Before the series, he lived in the east part of Greenwich Village in New York. Now he's taken an apartment in Hollywood. "I miss New York, but I'm beginning to like California," he said as he prepared to go back to work.

It was time for the bell to ring. Mr. Kotter was waiting.

What crazy story is Horshack coming up with now? Whatever it is, Mr. Kotter is willing to listen.

Lawrence-Hilton Jacobs:
The Cool Boom Boom Washington

Lawrence-Hilton Jacobs has wanted to be an actor for as long as he can remember. He was born in New York City, one of nine children. "We lived in a fairly poor area," Larry told me in an interview. "But there were people from different backgrounds and different social levels in the neighborhood. Growing up was really fun! I never went hungry. We all lived together. My father was in the Merchant Marine and traveled a great deal. He's retired now.

"Those days weren't always easy, though," Larry added. "I had great help from my brother who was 12 years older than I. He talked to me as a person. He and others helped give me confidence. A lot of kids don't have that direction. Some of my friends didn't end up well. I was lucky. I had art work I enjoyed and I played the piano. I played basketball. All of it was a learning process."

Larry has been working since he was 11 years old. His first job was washing stairways in an apartment building. "I did a lot of things," he recalled. "I delivered flowers and groceries. I was a messenger boy."

Larry liked art very much. "I went to the High School of Art and Design," he said. "I wanted to be a professional actor but that wasn't really possible then."

High school drama didn't appeal to him, however. "The drama class was a joke," he said. "After high school I was offered several scholarships, but I didn't want to go to college. I wanted to be an actor. I started acting with a group in Harlem and one thing led to another. I began to learn the business and get experience. I got into doing commercials. I graduated from high school in 1971. I got my first major job in 1973."

Larry worked hard, and his work has paid off. He believes that is very important. "I talk now to actors who don't think you have to study. You do! You must study and learn. And must be able to face discouragement. Sometimes I'd go on 20 auditions and not

An angry Boom Boom Washington (Lawrence-Hilton Jacobs) confronts Barbarino and Mr. Kotter between classes. Larry says that Boom Boom is less tough now than he was in the first few episodes of the show.

get a job. For seven months I tried to get parts in commercials. At the end of the day I'd ask myself: 'Why didn't I get that commercial?' Finally I began to understand myself, and I began to get parts in commercials. It doesn't take genius. It takes work."

His family wanted him to go to college. "They thought I was crazy!" Larry laughed. "I was thinking of something farfetched to them. Once I decided to be an actor, though, I decided to go all the way.

"I'm very serious about my life and my work," Larry said. "School was important to me. I knew the only person who could get me what I wanted was me. I'm serious. I'm strong in my beliefs. I have a lot of confidence, not because I'm brilliant but because I work. I went to classes, plays, films . . ."

Acting always looked like fun to him. "I was always clowning around," Larry said. "I put on puppet shows and so on. I'd see kids in films and thought it looked like fun. I was never in school plays, but I did church and community theater, off-Broadway, and Broadway.

Larry was in the films *Claudine* and *Cooley High*. "I also did *Sojourner Truth* on TV," he said. "I did about nine million commercials, voice overs, modeling work, stage plays . . . I tried every avenue that was open.

"The Kotter thing happened almost by accident," Larry explained. "I came out here to California to try out for a movie. They gave me a Kotter script and I met John Travolta. We read here. Then I went back to New York and did the screen test there."

He got the part of the tall, lean Boom Boom Washington. And he, like all the young people in the show, has added his own touches to the character.

"I can relate to Boom Boom," Larry said. "In junior high I played around a lot. I almost lived in the dean's office, in fact, because I like to play tricks on people.

"But I'm not really like Boom Boom. He's a character I play. Boom Boom goes to school only because there's nothing else to do. Then he meets Kotter — and he's the first teacher Boom Boom could ever relate to. Kotter's been there. These kids can learn from him. They get entertained and involved.

"I think kids can relate to the show," Larry continued. "It may get crazy at times, but the characters are real. There's not just one strong character on the show. They are *all* strong characters. That's unusual in TV comedy.

"And you can sit back and really laugh. Sometimes the writers write things that won't work for a character. When that happens we change the lines. At first my character was tough and threatening. I came up with the dancing stuff, the 'Mr. Kot-ter' stuff. I made a whole different character out of him. All of our characters are very different from when we started. The kids are still street-wise, but they're not threatening."

Larry sat at lunch looking very mod in a red warm-up suit and a beige hat. It was just the kind of outfit Boom Boom might have worn, in fact!

"I don't care about the whole Hollywood trip," he said. "I'm not in acting for the money. Sure, you need money to live, but I'm concerned about my work. I'm a very happy person. I see no reason to be sad. I have patience and I'm on the threshold of where I want to go as an actor. I know a lot about film and stage. TV is still new to me. I see a lot of great things happening in the future.

"The four of us on the show see each other very often," Larry added. "We might as well live together! John Travolta and I are especially good friends. We're greedy. We love to eat, so we go out a lot. I like junk food — pizza, hamburgers, etc. We also go to the movies quite often.

"The four of us and Gabe have all helped each other. Sometimes we worked on weekends to get a scene just right. What we have are people who care for each other on and off screen. That's what works for us."

John Travolta: Ba-ba-ba-barino

I first met John Travolta in the summer of 1975.

Kotter enjoys a quiet evening at home with his wife, Julie (Marcia Strassman).

Welcome Back, Kotter had not yet come on the air. ABC believed that John was a young actor with a great deal of appeal. They weren't so sure about the show's chances, but who could tell?

Who could tell, indeed? The show became a hit — and John Travolta, as Vinnie Barbarino, became a teen idol. And why not? Barbarino is the ringleader of the Sweathogs — and that takes special talent!

John was born in Englewood, New Jersey, one of six children of Helen and Salvatore Travolta. He started acting at the encouragement of his mother, who had been active as a teacher, director, and actress for 20 years.

"My father now owns a business in Hillsdale, New Jersey," John said. "At one time he was a semi-pro basketball player. My brothers were athletes. My father enjoyed all of our careers. He went to everything. Both my parents were interested in everything we did."

John quit high school in his junior year when he was 16 years old to become a full-time actor. "I was doing summer stock then, and I was working too much to go to school at the same time," he explained. "I enjoyed working. My mother understood. My three older sisters were all actresses and I had grown up watching them go through the problems of being actresses. I saw a lot of shows and

John Travolta was an experienced Broadway actor before he won the role of Vinnie Barbarino. Now *Welcome Back, Kotter* is a hit—and John's career is really taking off!

plays. It was a natural thing. Acting was all around me.

"I got involved in community theater as a child," John recalled. "When I was 14 I started going to New York to audition for professional parts. My first professional job was in summer stock in New Jersey. That was at the end of my sophomore year in high school." And that changed everything for John.

"Before that I lived a normal life. I had regular friends and buddies. We played sports. I played basketball and football from grades 7 to 10," John said.

But gradually he began to work more — and the jobs began to overlap with school. "I couldn't do both, and I wanted to work," John said. "My parents let me quit school. They understood what I wanted to do."

John got a job with a summer stock company in Pennsylvania and then played in a revival of *Rain* in an off-Broadway production. He was in the national touring company of *Grease*. "We traveled all over the country," he said. "I also did *Grease* on Broadway and was in *Over There* with the Andrews Sisters for nine months. That's enough for any one show!"

John moved to Los Angeles in 1972. He was 18 at the time. So far the best thing about his career, he said, "is that I've been able to get what I want out of life and I love that. I've always loved airplanes and now I have one. It's a two-seater Ercoupe.

"I have also bought my favorite kind of car in the whole world," John exclaimed. "It's a 1955 Thunderbird. Being an actor," he added, "is a well-rounded life. I have freedom to spend time with my plane and with people I like. I travel a lot and meet many people. Only through experience can you learn to deal with people.

"I've worked from the time I was 12. My first job was as a carpenter's helper. I put fabric on chairs and rebuilt tables."

I asked John if he thought there were disadvantages to having worked so much.

"I don't believe so," he answered. "When I was young, I always tried to have something going. When I wasn't playing basketball or acting or doing something, I fell apart. It's better to have something to do."

John believes the young people in *Kotter* are fairly true to life. "They harass the teacher and so on," he pointed out. "That's all part of school." John laughed. "I was an excellent ranker in school," he said. "I wasn't the champion, but I got a lot of laughs. I was something of a practical joker through school.

"I had one teacher like Mr. Kotter," John added. "That teacher was very funny. He communicated with us. He handled us, but with a sense of humor. We laughed, but we learned. Kotter is that kind of teacher.

"Some of the things we say on the show aren't quite what real kids would say," John pointed out. "But the Kotter kids are more believable than any other teenagers you see on TV."

Lindsay Wagner Leaps to Stardom as **The Bionic Woman**

The Bionic Woman was filming in Malibu Canyon the day I went out to see Lindsay Wagner. It was a breathtaking setting for a TV show: majestic mountains rose in the distance, a narrow road led to a stand of tall trees, and beside a running stream Lindsay and the camera crew were shooting a scene.

Soon after I arrived, the lunch break was called, and work stopped at once. Cast and crew had only 30 minutes for lunch, so there was no time to waste.

Lindsay and I walked to her trailer, one like those you see rolling down the highways in the summertime. The trailer was a place where Lindsay could go to rest when she wasn't working. Her secretary went to get lunch from a truck which had brought in hot and cold foods. There were no McDonald's Restaurants in this remote part of Malibu Canyon!

Lindsay had been working hard, but she didn't

Lovely Lindsay Wagner plays the part of superspy Jaime Sommers in the TV series, *The Bionic Woman*.

look tired. "The show is difficult," she admitted, as she settled down on a comfortable couch. "I do a lot of the running and jumping and the physical things myself. That makes it much harder. You wear yourself out!"

She smiled, and then added: "I had to spend several hours learning the mini-trampoline. They hide it behind a bush. Then I run, jump on it, and go over. It looks like I'm jumping in the air! Everything has been fairly easy and fun, though, even though I'm not really an athletic person."

Lindsay stars in a "fantasy hit" today, but admitted that she didn't like science fiction when she was younger. "I was a terrible realist," she laughed. "I didn't begin to like science fiction until I got older. I didn't fantasize as a kid. I wasn't really a kid until I was 20. Then I learned to have fun!"

Lindsay was born in Los Angeles. "I started modeling when I was 13," she recalled. "I was very tall and looked older than I really was. I was always around older people."

She also started taking dancing lessons when she was 13. She didn't do so well with those. First she tried ballet. "I'd been in the class two weeks when the teacher asked me if I'd like to try her jazz class. So I tried that. Then she asked me if I'd like to try modern dance. I finally said, 'Are you trying to tell me something?' She said, 'My husband has an acting class.' So

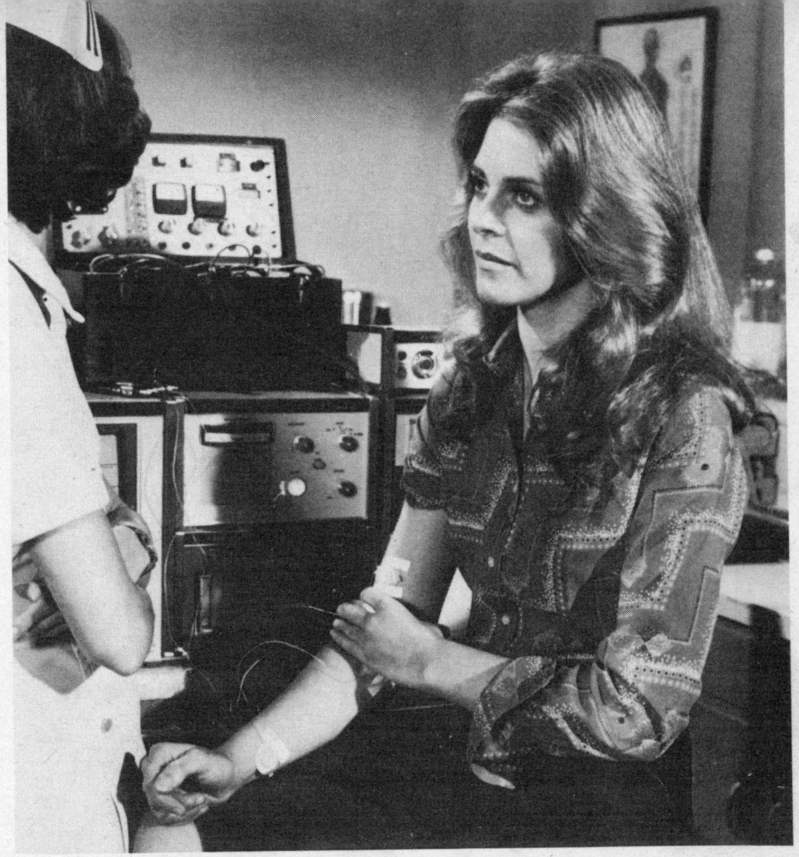

Even the health of a superstrong bionic woman must be checked sometimes—to make sure that all bionic parts are working correctly.

I got into acting! I was graceful when I was dancing, but I was a bit too stiff."

Acting was where she belonged. "It was perfect for me," Lindsay said. "I had been very withdrawn. But acting helped. When I was playing someone else, I could get my own emotions out."

Until acting came along, Lindsay had not had time

to have much fun. "I wasn't really very active in school," she explained. "I was always busy with other things. I took care of kids a lot — I spent the first half of my life baby-sitting! When I was only seven, I was taking care of my aunt's baby. Before my sister was born, I spent time raising Glen Campbell's first child. I was only 10 then! I didn't relate to kids who didn't have responsibilities. I couldn't get into playing. I never really had time to learn how!"

Then Lindsay moved to Portland, Oregon, with her mother and stepfather, and enrolled in David Douglas High School. Her mother tried to talk her into joining the high school drama class.

"I was terrible," Lindsay recalled with a smile. "I said, 'Oh, Mom, I've been working with professionals.' But one day I decided to give myself a good laugh. I went to the class, and to my surprise, the drama teacher was fantastic! I had really been wrong! I joined the class immediately."

Lindsay graduated from high school when she was 16. "Then I went to France for three months on an exchange program," she said. "When I came back I decided to go to college."

But after a year and a half of college, "I really wanted to get back to Los Angeles," Lindsay admitted. Finally she did come back and modeled for a year. Then "for several years I didn't do any modeling or any acting. I took other jobs. I sold clothes, I was a waitress, and so on. Finally I decided I was ready to take up my acting career. I was feeling good about myself and the time was right."

She called a friend who introduced her to the casting director at Universal Studios. And she got a part — 10 lines in a *Marcus Welby, M.D.* episode! Then everything began. Within seven months, she'd done guest spots in 12 TV shows and appeared in films.

Actually, Lindsay hadn't planned on doing a TV series. "Movies are my first love," she told me. But she was asked to play a bionic woman in an episode of *The Six Million Dollar Man* and almost turned it down! But it was her sister's favorite show, and her

A tough assignment for Jaime Sommers—in this episode, she had to somehow prevent the illegal sale of deadly weapons to a terrorist group.

sister's 13th birthday. "So I did the show and everything snowballed from there."

Nobody had intended to do a series about the bionic woman. In fact, they killed her off in that first show. "But after it was shown on TV, the mail poured in," Lindsay said. "People were very upset that they'd killed off the bionic woman."

So, because television audiences liked her so much, the producers did the only thing they could — they reached into the grab-bag of television fantasy and brought the bionic woman back to life!

How could Lindsay refuse to do the series? She couldn't.

Lindsay knows young people are a big part of her audience. "I can understand why," she said. "It's purely fantasy. Everyone wants to be superhuman. Everyone wants to have special powers. Kids today know about technology. They know bionics are real. Bionics don't give people the power that Jaime Sommers and Steve Austin have. But there really are artificial limbs that operate by muscle signals."

Jaime Sommers, the character Lindsay plays, is a teacher when she's not off using her bionic powers, and Lindsay herself once tried her hand at teaching. As for things in general, Lindsay says that this is a good time for her. "It's also a difficult time," she admitted. "This is a period of growth for me — and there is always both pain and joy to growth. You have to learn to cope," Lindsay added, "and so far I'm very happy with the way I've been getting along. I know I will look back on this as a happy time."

She currently shares her home with her pets: a horse named Lulu; a pure white mule named Nebbin; and two cats. She also likes to do needlepoint.

Opening a safe is as easy as one-two-three—if you happen to have bionic ears like Jaime Sommers!

Donny and Marie:
This Big Hit is a Family Affair

When I first met the Osmond family several years ago, the brothers were appearing at a big hotel in Hollywood, Florida. The two youngest Osmonds, Marie and Jimmy, hadn't yet joined the act. But now that they have, the group is better than ever.

This show business family still makes many personal appearances as a group and all of them are involved with Donny and Marie's hit TV show. It is one of the most original, exciting variety hours on the air. There are ice skating acts, trained animals, crazy dances — and all kinds of high jinks.

"We even had a TV first last year," Marie told me with a laugh. "You know how they throw a pie at a person? We threw a person at a pie! Do you know who it was?" I did, but I let her tell me.

"It was Donny!" she exclaimed. "We threw him into a huge pie filled with 96 gallons of whipped cream! My brothers pushed him in. After the show, they threw me in, too!" She laughed merrily.

All the Osmonds love their work. They don't fake enthusiasm. They are enthusiastic. Their schedule for eating and sleeping is sometimes turned upside down — but they're used to it!

Tracking them down for an interview isn't easy. Most recently, I caught them in Las Vegas where they were appearing in an act together. "Our whole family is here," Donny said. "We've been here about three weeks."

"Have you been having any fun?" I asked him.

"You bet!" Donny answered. "I've been out playing tennis and golf in the afternoons. And we're really having fun with the show! There's something for everybody in it."

"I just messed around today," Marie added. "I went shopping. Mainly I just looked around. I bought some make-up. Our first show isn't until 8:00 at night."

Their TV show was out of production right then, but Donny and Marie hadn't slowed down. "When we finish here, we'll go home to Utah for a few days," Donny explained. "Then Marie and I are doing a Bob Hope special."

"We'll do three of our own TV shows in July," Marie said. "Then the family is going on tour during August."

Donny and Marie Osmond are the young, vivacious co-hosts of their own exciting variety show, *Donny and Marie*.

I was dizzy just from hearing about their hectic lives. "But we like challenges," Donny hastened to tell me. "The TV show is really fun — and it's a lot of work. There's no other show like it — we've worked hard to come up with things that are new and different."

"We start our act here in Las Vegas with a four or five minute film clip of some of our TV shows," Marie said. "Sometimes we look at that film clip and say, 'Man, did we really learn all that dancing and all those songs?' "

"Our brothers are very much a part of the TV show," Donny pointed out. "It's really the *Osmond Show*, not just *Donny and Marie.* They are behind the scenes. Jay does all the choreography for us. All of them are involved in everything."

Donny and Marie are two of nine children. Marie is the only girl and loves it that way. "It's terrific!" she said. Her brothers are Virl, Tommy, Alan, Wayne, Merrill, Jay, Donny, and Jimmy. Only Virl and Tommy are not performing members of the family. Both have serious hearing problems and work in other areas of the family operation.

Marie was born in Ogden, Utah. She attended public school until the fourth grade. But once she began to travel with her family, she had to have tutors. "I'm in the 11th grade now," she told me. "When I was younger I was interested in secretarial

All the Osmonds are fantastic singers — and Donny and Marie are no exception! Here they perform one of their many show-stopping numbers.

work and I still am. I like business courses — typing, shorthand, all the business things. My mother was a secretary, so she's helped me a lot."

Marie has recorded three singles and three albums. They are "Paper Roses," "In My Little Corner of the World," and "Who's Sorry Now?" Donny and Marie have also recorded three singles together:

"I'm Leaving It All Up to You," "Make the World Go Away," and "Morning Side of the Mountain."

In the show Marie has added a country music song to her brothers' act. "How did that happen?" I asked her.

"You know, it's funny," she replied. "When I started singing, no matter what I sang it had a country flavor to it. When I went to Nashville, they said, 'Try some country music.' I sing more country pop. I just enjoy it — and nobody else in the family sang that way. We like to take advantage of opportunities!"

The Osmonds are members of the Church of Jesus Christ of the Latter-Day Saints (Mormons). Marie is involved in their MIA (Mutual Improvement Association) program with other girls her age. Her hobbies are making clothes, designing, and cooking. "When we're here in Las Vegas," she added, "I play tennis and go out to the pool. It's really nice being here for three weeks. But that's long enough. We're free all day — it's hard to take that for too long a time."

Marie is 16 years old. "And we're allowed to date when we're 16," she said. "I've been out on some dates but you can't really date when you're on tour. The girls scream at Donny," she added with a laugh. "But boys don't scream, so I don't have that problem."

Donny is 18. "I graduated from high school last spring," he said proudly.

"He's a big man now," Marie added.

"I'm finished having tutors now, which is nice," Donny continued. "Now I'm going to take a correspondence course in electronics."

Donny was four years old when he was introduced on *The Andy Williams Show*. He was a big hit doing an imitation of Andy singing "You Are My Sunshine."

He's been performing ever since. To an outsider, it doesn't always look like an easy life. When they are on the road, they must be very careful on leaving or entering their hotel rooms. Young fans swarm throughout the lobbies of the hotel where the Osmonds are appearing, hoping to get a glimpse of their idols. The hotel switchboards are forced to cut off all calls into their suite of rooms.

"We sneak out, though," Donny said. "Sometimes we use the service elevator. Then we go out the back entrance through the kitchen and the garage. But we don't mind. It's our business. You sacrifice quite a bit of your private life. But it's neat to have girls chase you!" he added with a laugh. "It keeps things interesting."

The Osmonds do two shows a night when they are on tour. The last one is usually just beginning at about 12:30 a.m. I asked them how they managed to eat and sleep. "It's not so bad," said Donny. "We just switch our hours. You can get eight hours of

Costumes and comedy add to the all-around merriment of the show. Here Donny spoofs the nifty Fifties, a liontamer's job, Superman, and—best of all—Clark Kent!

sleep even if you go to bed at 3:00 a.m. or so. We don't like to eat before a show, so we have dinner about 2:00 a.m."

"We live out of suitcases, but we consider Utah our home," Donny said.

It was there that they were schooled in the tradition of the Mormon Church. "It was because of the church that we started singing together," Donny said.

The other brothers had gathered around during my chat with Donny and Marie. "Our church emphasizes families working together," Alan told me. "Once a week our family would have an especially nice dinner. After the meal each of us would have to get up and perform. We could do anything — sing, recite, tell what happened in school. I played bass violin in school, but singing was easier for us. During the week our mother would teach us a song for the next week. We sang at church, at birthday parties, and other places. Our mother taught us harmony and how to read music. She also taught us how to play sax. She was in the band in high school and college. Our father was in a choral group."

Early in their career, the group appeared with Andy Williams on his TV show and in concerts. "But we wanted to get out on our own, and Andy gave us his blessing," Alan recalled. "We hadn't been confirmed for the Andy Williams TV show when we went to Los Angeles, but we felt we had to try it. Andy's father heard us singing at Disneyland. We reminded him of *his* boys. That led to our contract with Andy."

"Lawrence Welk wouldn't take us once," Jay said, and they all laughed.

The Osmonds' sound has changed a great deal in recent years. "We started out in the barbershop vein," older brother Alan told me. "But we've broadened. The group has to keep moving. We don't want all our songs to sound the same."

Yes, they are an amazing family. They have many interests. But mostly they are involved with their music. They love to perform and they intend to keep it up. They're in harmony — on stage and off. Donny and Marie are big hits on TV and the people who are helping them the most — and applauding the loudest — are their own family.

An Unusual TV Series About a Crazy Police Department: **Barney Miller**

Barney Miller really is an unusual TV police show. It is a cop show without violence and it's also one of the funniest, best-written shows on TV.

The cops in *Barney Miller* are like the doctors in *M*A*S*H*. Danger may be all around them, but they can still laugh and cut up and have a good time.

Barney is a captain of detectives at New York's 12th Precinct house in Greenwich Village. His squad room is staffed with all types of people. It is a melting pot of craziness.

The show came on ABC several years ago as a mid-season replacement. From the very first, it was different — and nobody watched it. The ratings were terrible. But the few people who did watch it talked about it. Word-of-mouth reports began to spread. A station manager in New England wrote ABC: "I don't

Hal Linden was a perfect choice for the role of *Barney Miller*—the calm, compassionate Chief of Detectives at the 12th precinct house.

care what the numbers (of viewers) are. We need this show to give the network class."

Letters began to arrive from real-life policemen and their families. A letter from the Detroit Police Department's 12th Precinct noted: "The working conditions and characters shown in your program can be fairly well duplicated in our office. We laugh so much at times that it hurts." One young fan wrote, "My father's police department is as crazy as yours."

ABC wisely decided to stick with the show. Its

number of viewers began to increase. "It's the one show I try never to miss," one fan told me.

"I think *Barney Miller* is much more real than any other cop show on TV," Gregory Sierra told me. Gregory played a detective named Chano in the show for several seasons. "The people in the show have real problems," he pointed out. "They worry about things. Kojak never worries. He knows he's got it made. Everything is always under control on that show. You never see the frustrations of police work or the kind of joking that goes on among real policemen. Those are the kinds of things shown on *Barney Miller*.

"I was talking to a California highway patrolman not long ago," Gregory said. "He told me they joke and carry on. You have to. When you're dealing with life-and-death situations, you can't be deadly serious all the time or you'd go crazy."

Hal Linden, who plays Barney Miller, has been a performer since he was a teenager. "Being in this series has done wonders for me and for my career," Hal said in an interview. "There are so many things I want to do. I hope this series will make them possible. There were many years when I couldn't get the jobs I wanted."

Hal began his career playing the saxophone and singing. "I started as a kid musician," he remembered. "I was 13 when I started playing at local

Fish (Abe Vigoda) anxiously waits to hear the results of a phone call that could mean another, easier job for him. But would Fish really leave the detective squad?

dances for $2.00 a night. I joined the musicians' union at the age of 15."

Hal grew up in New York City. "I went to the High School of Music and Art," he said. "Those teen years were painful times. We were a lower-middle-class family. My father was a printer. Even in the worst of times, though, my parents gave me music lessons. Music was very important to me. I didn't play sports much. I used music as a way of meeting people. I would go to dances and play in the band. That way I didn't have to dance! I was very shy."

Hal majored in music at Queens College and graduated with a degree in business from City College, New York. He was touring as a saxophone player and singer with Sammy Kaye when the Korean War broke out. He was drafted, but he didn't leave his music behind. He became a member of the U.S. Army Band and also acted in army shows. How did the shy musician take to acting? Like a duck to water!

After his discharge from the army, he enrolled at New York's American Theatre Wing. He studied acting there for a year. In 1958, he got his first big break. He was signed to understudy Sydney Chaplin in the musical comedy *Bells Are Ringing* on Broadway. Five days after joining the show, he got a chance to show what he could do. He went on in the leading role and eventually replaced Chaplin, co-starring with Judy Holliday in New York and on tour in the national company.

He thought he had it made. "But then nothing happened in my career until 1966!" Hal admitted. "I had seven years of famine! Those were depressing years. At times I wondered why I kept trying."

But he did keep trying. By 1966, he was beginning to get good roles in Broadway shows. Finally, he was on his way. He got the starring role in *The*

Rothschilds on Broadway and won a Tony Award, Broadway's highest honor. Then he came to the attention of TV producer Danny Arnold. Danny Arnold just happened to be casting a show he had created called *Barney Miller*. He decided that Hal Linden would be perfect in the title role. And Danny Arnold was absolutely right.

Barney Miller is the voice of sanity in the chorus of craziness. Fish is fighting with his wife. . . . Wojehowicz is afraid to fly. . . . Snipers are shooting at policemen. . . . Barney takes it all in stride.

Each show features a steady parade of offbeat characters through the station house. Sometimes their problems are serious, sometimes they aren't. But somehow, no matter what happens, the problems always end up being funny.

One night a man went into the station house and told Fish that terrible things were happening to his marriage. (Fish often says that about his own marriage!) In this case, the man's wife had taken all their savings and used them to book passage for a trip — to outer space. She'd been sold a high-priced ticket to nowhere, the man was convinced, and he wanted to get the salesman who had played the dirty trick. Fish may have considered sending his own wife on the same trip — but he finally managed to get the whole problem settled. The trip was called off.

The team at work. Fish explains a report to boss Barney Miller as a confused Wojo (Max Gail) tries to understand.

While Fish was busy inside the station house, Wojo (Wojehowicz's nickname) was outside — being shot at by a sniper. "Why me?" Wojo wondered. Then the big brass of the police department arrived to help in the capture. It never took place, but at least the sniper moved into another neighborhood, which made Wojo feel better.

Hal Linden says that he wants to be as believable as possible in the role of Barney Miller.

Craziness? Well, it's a crazy world. There are horse thieves, con men, pickpockets, and all sorts of ragtag people down on their luck. They all seem to end up with Barney Miller and his gang in the 12th Precinct house — and that changes everything for them.

"The best thing about the show is that anything can happen," Hal pointed out. "It's really become a play about a place rather than any one person. The place takes over rather than the characters.

"The character of Barney Miller," Hal continued, "is a combination of all the good things I would like to have in my own personality. I think his biggest asset is his compassion. He tries to bring out the positive side of everybody."

Hal smiled. "I don't know if Barney is human. I guess he's a little superhuman. We don't want him to seem too perfect, though, or he wouldn't be believable."

Hal has settled in for a long run in one of TV's wackiest — and best — shows. So have his fellow TV cops: Abe Vigoda as the tired, sad-faced Fish; Max Gail as the easygoing, gum-chewing Wojehowicz; Jack Soo as Nick; and Ron Glass as Harris.

Barney Miller is a team effort — and what a team! They really make it work. Imagine — a cop show with no gun fights, no bloody bodies, no screaming auto chases. That's *Barney Miller!*

Mike Farrell: **M*A*S*H**'s Great New Face

It isn't easy to be the new kid in town. Everybody else knows each other. You're the outsider.

Mike Farrell felt a little like that when he joined the cast of *M*A*S*H*. The show was already a big hit. Everybody knew everybody and the parts they were playing. Mike was to be a young doctor, newly arrived in Korea. He was to fill the gap left when Wayne Rogers quit his Trapper John role. It was a juicy assignment — but a challenging one. Mike didn't want to have to fill Wayne Rogers' shoes. He would have to create his own character — and establish his own identity.

"And I loved it from the very first," Mike said in an interview. "Working with Alan Alda (who plays Hawkeye) is a dream. I wouldn't have wanted to step into someone else's role and they didn't ask me to. Before I took the role, I wanted to make sure I would be a useful person on the show. And I wanted to make sure there were no prior conditions to the character that I wouldn't like. I was reassured on all points."

Getting a role on *M*A*S*H* was a big break for Mike, though his career was already perking briskly.

"I had been under contract to Universal for four years," Mike said. "I was quite comfortable. There were no restrictions on whether I worked or not. I had been establishing a place in town. The next logical step was for me to be the lead in my own series. And here I was being asked to step into a long-running series and be in the second slot behind Alan Alda. From a career point of view, it was a question of whether I should do *M*A*S*H* or wait for my own series." *M*A*S*H* won out. Mike joined the medics in Korea in the role of B.J. Hunnicutt.

"I've wanted to be an actor since I was 10 years old," Mike recalled. "I was taken with the whole idea of movies, stardom, fame, and all the rest." Mike laughed. "I had this idea of being famous , but I had no earthly idea of how it would happen! I guess I thought someone would tap me on the shoulder and that would be it! I never took a drama class in high school. I took a speech class and I was dreadfully afraid."

Mike went to Hollywood High School. "I suppose I would have been described by others as being a popular, well-adjusted, good student," he noted. "I realize now that I was anything but that. I was kind of an over-achiever acting out a role. It was my way of reacting to all the pressures. In my family we were expected to maintain a very rigid set of standards. A lot of them were not really spelled out. We were just expected to know what to do. That wasn't easy for my brother and two sisters and me."

B.J. Hunnicutt (Mike Farrell) and Hawkeye Pierce (Alan Alda) are close friends as well as tentmates. Mike says he really likes working with Alan Alda.

Hot Lips (Loretta Swit) tries to convince Hawkeye and B.J. that it's against army regulations to use the M*A*S*H phone for personal calls to their families in the United States.

Mike was in the Marine Corps for two years after high school graduation. "I was in Okinawa, Japan, San Diego, and so on," he said. "I hated it. After I got out of the service, I did all kinds of odd jobs, including driving a truck and cooking in a restaurant. But one day I was talking to a friend about being an actor and he said: 'If you want to be an actor, you better do something about it.' "

Mike began to study drama at Los Angeles City College and at UCLA. He was studying at the Jeff Corey Workshop in Hollywood in 1961 when he got his first professional job in a little theater production of *Rain*. It was a start, and it led to roles in several movies, including *The Graduate*.

Mike Farrell has really added his own charm and sensitivity to the role of combat surgeon B.J. Hunnicutt. M*A*S*H is lucky to have him!

Here, B.J. Hunnicutt has just arrived at M*A*S*H (that's why he's all dressed up). Sharing a relaxing moment with him at the Officer's Club are Radar (Gary Burghoff) and Hawkeye (Alan Alda).

Gradually, Mike began to get bigger and better roles. "I suppose my first real break came in 1968," Mike said. He was cast as a regular on the daytime series *Days of Our Lives*. Then came a regular role in *The Interns,* followed by the *Man and the City* series.

Like Hunnicutt, Mike is married. In real life his wife is actress Judy Farrell, whom he met in a musical-comedy class at UCLA. They have two children: Josh, 7, and Erin, 4.

"Judy is such a good actress," Mike said proudly. "But it's tougher to be an actress than an actor. There are many fewer roles for women than for men."

The Farrells live in Sherman Oaks, California, and Mike hates being away from his family for very long at a time. "When I'm away for five days it seems like a century!" he laughed.

Mike is no longer a new face on *M*A*S*H*. He settled into the role of combat surgeon with ease. But he isn't another Wayne Rogers or Trapper John. He is himself — with his own charm and sensitivity — and somehow, now it seems as though B.J. Hunnicutt has always been with the 4077th.

A Brand-New Kind of Science Fiction Show: **Space: 1999**

Moonbase Alpha has been spinning around in outer space for more than a year now. Moonbase Alpha, as most sci-fi fans know, is the setting for *Space: 1999*, a weekly TV series that comes up with some really far-out adventures.

Barbara Bain and Martin Landau star in the series. They play Dr. Helena Russell and Commander John Koenig, the two most important people on Moonbase Alpha. The show also added a new character during its second season. She's a strange alien who can change herself into an animal, a bird, or any other creature! (*Star Trek*'s Vulcan, Mr. Spock, has pointed ears, and alien powers can make his behavior change, but Spock keeps his own shape — he can't change himself into a bird!) The new alien in *Space: 1999* is played by Catherine Schell, who starred with Peter Sellers in the movie *The Return of the Pink Panther*.

Space: 1999 began with a series of man-made disasters. Moonbase Alpha had been set up on the surface of the moon. On it were over 300 men and women from many nations of the world. They had been sent there to do research. They hadn't planned on staying there forever. Their plans didn't work out, however.

Back on Earth, atomic power had become the major source of man's energy needs. And getting rid of the atomic waste had become a big problem. The Earthlings had to find something to do with it — so they decided to ship it into outer space and store it on the far side of the moon.

That's a fine idea if you yourself don't happen to be living on the moon. As more and more waste was put on the moon, dangerous reactions from it began. Finally, a series of explosions occurred that tore away portions of the moon. The moon, with Moonbase Alpha still on it, was blasted out of Earth's orbit. Now it is moving away from Earth and nothing can stop it!

"We never get back in touch with Earth as we know it," Martin Landau told me in an interview. "There we are, headed further out into space. We have no business being out there. We weren't prepared for such a journey. We hadn't planned on spending the rest of our lives together! We have a life-support system, but it doesn't allow for anything extra. We can just about keep ourselves alive!"

During its first season, Moonbase Alpha ran into all kinds of exciting adventures — from alien space beings to hostile environments. It got caught in blinding snowstorms and in interplanetary wars. It was attacked by unfamiliar illnesses and by strange-looking "people." Catherine Schell, as the new alien who was taken on board, is the daughter of a mad scientist. The scientist's planet had been destroyed. He hoped to rebuild it with the minds of the residents of Moonbase Alpha. He had his test tubes bubbling away and was all set. Luckily, he was stopped in time — and *Space: 1999* is blasting off for a second season.

Commander John Koenig (Martin Landau) is the leader of the Moonbase Alpha colony. It's not an easy job — the survival of 300 people depends on him!

Dr. Helena Russell (Barbara Bain) is Chief Medical Officer. She's in charge of all life support systems—everything that has to do with the general health and well-being of the colony's human and plant life.

"Could any of this happen in real life?" I asked Martin Landau and Barbara Bain, who are husband and wife in their own "real" lives. Martin smiled. "It's possible that we might use the moon as a nuclear waste dump," he replied. "It's a logical place. A shuttle bus could run back and forth between the moon and the Earth. It's also possible that life exists in outer space in some shape or form."

Barbara Bain agreed with her husband. "It would be very conceited of us to think we humans are the only form of life," she added. "There are so many possibilities. Who's to say that there aren't other beings living in totally different environments?"

Space: 1999 has made a big splash around the

A scouting party checks out the complicated security system that surrounds the colony. A ring of fences and photoelectric "fields" runs for twenty miles around the compound. This system keeps out intruders.

Catherine Schell plays Maya, the daughter of a mad scientist. She has made the moonbase her home. Maya can actually change herself into any creature she wants to be!

world — the world we know, that is! "We are riding the crest of a huge wave of interest in science fiction," said one spokesman for the series. "And there is a worldwide appetite for TV shows that are different. That is why we spent more than seven million on new shows for the second season."

"Working on this series has been an incredible experience," Martin Landau told me. "Most science fiction deals with people running around in Buck Rogers suits looking silly," he said. "Our shows are more involved and more imaginative. They don't take place too many years into the future. We have today's viewpoints and emotions. Yet we come into contact with civilizations that are millions and mil-

In this episode, the people of Moonbase Alpha had to somehow defend themselves from an attack by a huge spaceship of deadly aliens!

Dr. Russell (Barbara Bain) and Commander Koenig (Martin Landau) are constantly facing dangers from the farthest limits of Outer Space.

lions of years ahead of us. And we find that some of them don't want us on their planets!"

Loyal "Trekkies," who may have felt that *Star Trek* had a warmth and spark that was missing in *Space: 1999*, should like the show better this year; the *Space: 1999* producers have tried to inject more "human-ness" into the series, and lessen the cold, purely scientific atmosphere of the earlier shows.

Space: 1999 is not on one of the major networks. But it is shown by more than 100 stations in the U.S. and in more than 100 countries around the world. Often it has more viewers than the network shows.

"The shows are produced in London," Martin said. "Nothing is spared in either time or money."

England, he might have added, is where modern outer space science fiction really began — with H.G. Wells' terrifying story, *The War of the Worlds*.

The people on Moonbase Alpha have had some exciting and dangerous times. But for most of them, whirling around in outer space hasn't been such a bad adventure after all!

Starsky and Hutch:
TV's Exciting *New* Undercover Team

TV didn't need a new cop show. It was already filled with policemen of all kinds. But ABC went ahead with plans for a new show called *Starsky and Hutch*. "It's going to be a big hit," they kept saying.

Surprisingly, they were right. It didn't take long for Starsky and Hutch to become TV's hottest new team. They hit the screen with tires squealing. And they haven't slowed down much since then.

The two men are plainclothes policemen. "I'm glad you guys work the street," their captain growls. "You look lousy in uniforms."

What does the show offer that other police shows don't? Paul Michael Glaser (Starsky) and David Soul (Hutch) are often asked that question. To them, the answer is simple. Paul says, "What we have is a special chemistry between two people."

Starsky and Hutch get along. They are alike in certain ways but they are also quite different. Dark-haired Starsky looks like a street fighter. Tall, blond Hutch looks like a surfer.

Starsky is the one who drives the red Ford at high speeds. Sometimes he goes the wrong way on one-way streets.

I met Paul Glaser and David Soul last summer. Their show was about to go into production for a second season. Both had been busy working on other projects but they were eager to get back to *Starsky and Hutch*.

Paul came into the interview wearing a yellow leather-like jacket and sunglasses pushed up into his dark hair. He is intense and intelligent. He has been called — and has called himself — "an angry young man." He is also thoughtful, concerned, and very aware of the people around him.

"I think our show has many strengths," he said. "Obviously a big part of its appeal is the relationship between Starsky and Hutch. They are two people who care for each other very much. They would lay down their lives for each other. You put people like that in exciting, dangerous situations — and you can come up with some very exciting stories."

Paul had a rough first year on *Starsky and Hutch*. "You could divide my first season into two parts," he said. "At first I wasn't sure people would understand me. I fought a lot then — not physically, but for the

Paul Michael Glaser and David Soul are *Starsky and Hutch* —a series about a plainclothes police team. They get the toughest cases and work the roughest beat in town.

things I believed in. Then I began to realize that there are limitations to TV — and that everyone was working together. I began to trust my fellow workers more. I began to learn what I could expect from them and from myself. I began to relax."

"What were some of the battles over?" I asked Paul.

"We weren't really fighting about the characters of Starsky and Hutch," he replied. "Mainly we were quarreling over the development of stories and ideas. You constantly have to learn. Probably the best thing about doing a show like this isn't what you see on the TV screen. For the actor, it's the communication between all the people who put that show together. I had to learn that."

There may have been disagreements behind the scenes. There are on most shows. But *Starsky and Hutch* became a runaway hit. "It's a lot of work," Paul pointed out. "But I'm so much more in touch with myself now than I was before. It's incredible! When something like this happens to you, all of a sudden you're in the public eye. You have to be responsible for what you do and what you say. You find yourself being much more selective with your life."

Being a TV star can have its drawbacks, but they don't bother Paul. "Probably the only thing you lose is a degree of privacy," he said. "I don't worry about that. It's been a marvelous, amazing experience," he added. "You smarten up a lot! You learn a lot about people."

Paul was born in Cambridge, Massachusetts, on March 25, 1943. "I was a very angry kid," he recalled. "As a child, I was never able to express who I was, how I felt about things, how the world affected me. I went to a coed boarding school, but I commuted, so I kept very much to myself. I drove back and forth in sort of a hot rod. It wasn't considered a hot rod back in my hometown, but it was at that school! Ninety percent of the kids were walking around with long hair and guitars. I had some friends at school and at home, but they weren't really close friends."

Paul doesn't grant many interviews. He's tired of talking about himself. He had agreed to this interview because it was for young people — and he hasn't forgotten what it was like to be young!

"One thing I'd like kids to know," he stressed, "is that I had a very painful childhood. I'm saying to them: You have a painful childhood and I know what that's like — the loneliness and the sense of isolation.

"I understand what young people are going through. When I see kids today, I say, 'Do you have any good teachers?' That makes such a difference!

"I had three good teachers in high school. Then I

Starsky (far right) and Hutch (center) listen carefully as Huggy Bear (Antonio Fargas, left) gives them vital information that could help them to find a stolen car filled with 200 pounds of dynamite!

decided to go to college. It seemed to be the thing to do. My father was an architect. He had gone to college. My sisters had gone to college. So I went to college. It seemed like a great waste of time and money, but I guess I needed that experience."

Paul attended Tulane University in New Orleans. He graduated as a theater and English major. From there he went to Boston University, where he earned a Master's Degree in acting and directing. While he was going to school in Boston, he did several seasons in summer stock theaters before starting out in New York City.

Paul first appeared on stage when he was four years old. "I got up on a pillow in the living room, turned on the radio, and pretended I was conducting the Boston Symphony Orchestra," he recalled with a smile. "Then I was in *Amahl and the Night Visitors* when I was about 14.

"I don't think I ever really decided to be an actor," Paul said. "I looked for a college with a good theater arts department, but I don't think I'd really made the choice. It was a dream. I loved Humphrey Bogart, Gary Cooper, and Clark Gable. I watched a lot of movies and a lot of TV. I spent a lot of time by myself with my fantasies. I'd go hunting and spend the day walking through the woods. Fantasies are strange things," he added with a grin.

"I used to think that if I counted to 26 every night when I went to bed, then when I got to be 26 years old, I'd never get any older. In my fantasies I wanted to be a great hunter and a great everything! I wanted attention, love, affection — all of that went along with my fantasies."

Paul made his New York stage debut in a rock version of *Hamlet* in 1968. He was a regular in two daytime TV series: *Love of Life* and *Love Is a Many Splendored Thing*. He also appeared in several plays on Broadway.

"I have just finished doing a TV movie about the magician Houdini," Paul remarked wryly. "When I started the film I was very cocky. I said, 'Oh, I know how to do all of this.' And that first week was terrible!

I *didn't* know it all! But we're always growing. But on the whole today is a happy time," Paul said. "All of this is just the beginning of what I hope to do. I'd like to direct a great movie. I'd like to do things that will really reach the people and pick them up."

And what about all the fancy driving on the show, I asked Paul. Does he do any of it?

"Yes, I do," he replied. "I do a lot of the driving on the show, though they won't let me do the really dangerous stuff. I drove a lot as a teenager. That's where I learned."

When he's not working, Paul said, "I go to the beach or to the movies. I play tennis. I take my two dogs for long walks. And recently," he added, "I sang for the first time at a benefit with David (Soul). Was that fun!"

* * *

David Soul, who plays the tough, but soft-spoken Ken Hutchinson in *Starsky and Hutch,* was born David Solberg. His father is a Lutheran minister, a professor of history, and a former religious affairs adviser for the U.S. State Department.

"My father never had a church of his own," David told me. "We lived in South Dakota. He filled in. There were many churches out in the wilds that didn't have ministers. Dad taught college during the week. Then on weekends he would go around to three or four different churches. The family went

Tension builds as Starsky and Hutch learn that their lives are in danger because someone at headquarters has "leaked out" news of their secret mission to the criminal they are seeking.

with him. The churches were all within about 50 miles of home."

Twice the family went to Europe to live. "That was when my father was working for the government," David said. "I was six the first time we went to Europe and about 12 the second time. There was a real feeling of adventure in my family. I think that was what was terrific about the whole thing. We were a big family and we always moved together. Those two opportunities to go to Europe were fantastic. And I made friends very easily."

There were five children in his family, David said. All of them are in different careers now. "The only thing our parents stressed was that whatever we do, we do it well,'' he said.

David was a political science major in college. He went to Augustana College in Sioux Falls, South Dakota, the University of the Americas in Mexico City, and the University of Minnesota. ''When I was young, political science, German, baseball, and teaching were my interests,'' he said. ''I wanted to teach political science and history.''

But somewhere along the way, he recalled, ''Someone gave me a guitar and I learned to play music and sing.''

Music began to be more and more important to him. ''Finally, I decided I had to get out of the Midwest,'' he said. ''I'd done everything I could in terms of music. I'd done college concerts and so on. I'd gone through three years of college. The first two years I got straight A's; the third year I failed every course.

''I was at the University of Minnesota then. Nothing in me wanted to study. I wanted to sing and to act.''

He decided New York was the place to be. ''I had no friends there and little money. I look back,'' he added, shaking his head, ''and think, 'The nerve of that kid!' I can't believe I went there like that! I had worked as a cowboy in Montana that spring, so I had cowboy boots and short jeans. I arrived in New York looking like the Midnight Cowboy. I had a suitcase and a cardboard box with string tied around it. Somebody at home had told me about a lawyer, so I called him. I slept on his couch for two months while I tried to get started."

His way of getting started was most unusual, to say the least. He'd gotten the idea before he had left the Midwest. He'd call himself The Covered Man, he had decided. "It was a gimmick I used," David said with a smile. "I put a bag over my head and cut out two eyes and a nose. Then I took my picture and sent it to New York along with a tape recording of my singing. I didn't take the bag off in public for the first four months I was in New York."

Did the gimmick work? "You'd be surprised how much this business is run by curiosity!" David replied. He finally took the paper bag off — and ended up making 26 appearances on *The Merv Griffin Show*.

"I also worked as a stand-in for game shows," he noted. "I made enough to pay for acting lessons and an apartment. It was a great time! A casting director saw me on the Griffin show and I was signed to a contract at Columbia Screen Gems. I came out here to California on their New Talent Program, which doesn't exist any more. The idea had been to develop new talent through workshops and so on."

Several years ago, David landed a starring role in

an ABC series called *Here Come the Brides.* "I played a lumberjack," he said. "Then, after that, I couldn't get a job for two and a half years. I guess that was because people identified me with the role I played on that show. The role didn't give me a chance to show I could act. About all I did was smile and be charming."

So he had a couple of rough years. "But I stayed here," David said. "That's the only way to do it. I built a theater. I wrote music. I was in three or four plays — and I did a lot of homework!"

Finally, a Hollywood writer-producer named William Blinn wrote a screenplay for an *ABC Movie of the Week.* He called it *Starsky and Hutch.* The two heroes were to be "two interesting guys, dressed like a couple of dropouts, racing around in a bright red car...and who, despite their manner and appearance, were very good cops working the roughest, toughest beat in town."

David Soul was signed to play Hutch. But finding Starsky took longer. Dozens of actors were interviewed. Paul Michael Glaser was finally chosen for the part. The producers had the team they wanted. "I would like to have played Starsky," David admitted.

"As an actor, I've always found it easier to hide behind a character. Hutch is more like me than Starsky is. Starsky is quite different from me. He's a little more brassy."

David doesn't question the success of the team that was selected, however. He and Paul Michael Glaser have known each other since 1967. They agree completely on the direction in which they would like their show and their characters to go.

"It's hard to define where you want something to go," David said. "But wherever it is Paul and I agree

Starsky (Paul Glaser, right) and Hutch (David Soul, left) like to be on top of things! Paul and David both feel that the close friendship of the two characters is one of the most important things about the show.

on it. We want the show to continue to grow and develop. We'd like to see more humor in it."

Has success spoiled the life-style of the former Covered Man? David smiled. "I guess so," he answered. "People are always changing. But I think it's marvelous! It's allowed me to be more selective and to have faith in what I believe in. Before, I might have backed off if I had an idea. Now I don't. It's like someone told me about my music. If you're going to sing someone else's stupid lyrics, you might as well sing your own stupid lyrics! All of this has given me confidence in the way *I* think.

"You must avoid the traps, though," David pointed out. "I'm in a hit series now. Everybody is patting me on the back. I have to make sure that my work is good enough and varied enough so that I can continue to do what I love to do — and not be limited by a show. I want to develop as an actor.

"Listen," David said intently, "a series is here today and gone tomorrow. What's left then is *you*. You've got to do what you can now to buy time and space down the line. I chose to be an actor 12 years ago. In doing so, it became my whole life. All I've done up to this point is make myself ready for this moment."

David had kept busy while the series was out of production. He had been in an ABC movie called *Little Ladies of the Night*. "And I just finished my first album," he said proudly. "All of the songs on it are my own. I'm very serious about my music," he added. "I want to make it as good as I possibly can. As soon as the album comes out, I'd like to take a show out on the road — a kind of multi-media musical.

"There is still so much to do," David said enthusiastically. "It's like I really can't wait for every day to start."

But when he's not working? "I skin-dive, water-ski, ride horses, play tennis, and run a lot," he said. "I'm going to Baja California for five days to do all of that. I'm in the worst physical shape I've ever been in. I need a rest!"

A five day rest, maybe. But chances are, David Soul will be ready to go back to work before the five days are up. He's had to work hard — and wait patiently — to reach this point in his career, and as he said, there is still much to be done.

Mackenzie Phillips and Valerie Bertinelli Take Things **One Day at a Time**

Not too long ago, I began to get a lot of mail about two girls named Mackenzie Phillips and Valerie Bertinelli. The two teenagers were starring in a CBS series called *One Day at a Time*. Viewers wondered who they were. What had they done before? I couldn't answer their questions. I hadn't met the girls. Finally I decided it was time to change all that and I headed for Los Angeles to meet them. Want to come along? I think you'll like them!

* * *

Mackenzie Phillips (Julie Cooper in *One Day at a Time*) was sitting calmly at a table in the Beverly Wilshire Hotel when I arrived. I was surprised when I saw her. Mackenzie is much prettier than she appears to be in the role of Julie Cooper. She laughed when I mentioned it. "I just curled my hair," she exclaimed. Her hair was short and curly and looked great.

Mackenzie has several claims to fame. At the age

of 17 (she was born November 10, 1959), she is one of the stars of a TV comedy hit. Her father is singer-composer John Phillips, a member of the once-popular singing group The Mamas and Papas. Way back in her family there is even a "skeleton in the closet" — or at least a relative with quite a reputation: a gangster of the 1930's named Pretty Boy Floyd.

Barbara, her sister Julie (Valerie Bertinelli and Mackenzie Phillips, left) and their mother, Ann (Bonnie Franklin, far right) can always count on a good wisecrack from their funny, loveable neighbor and friend, David (Richard Masur, center).

Mackenzie lives with her aunt Rosie and cousin Nancy. Her family is scattered in all directions. "But we keep in touch," she said. "My father is in London now working on a film. My mother and brother Jeffrey live in the San Fernando Valley. I love my parents dearly," Mackenzie added. "My aunt Rosie is also like a mother to me. She is very understanding and very loving."

Mackenzie is in the 11th grade at the Hollywood Professional School. She didn't really set out to be an actress. "A group of us at school got together and formed a band," she said. "We started writing songs and rehearsing every day. One night, I was singing lead for the band during amateur night at the Troubador cafe. There was a casting director in the audience. He wanted to cast me for a part in the movie *American Graffiti*. I said, 'Okay, I'll do it.' I guess it was after that movie that I realized I wanted to be an actress.

"I've never taken an acting lesson," Mackenzie admitted. "I never felt the need to. I'm sure a demanding part will come along, though, that I'll need to be coached for."

So far her most demanding role, Mackenzie said, "was playing Eleanor Roosevelt as a young woman in *Eleanor and Franklin* on ABC. I played her until she was about 16. Then Jane Alexander played her as an adult. My grandmother told me a lot about

A talented singer as well as an actress, Mackenzie Phillips was picked for the role of Julie Cooper after she had appeared in a major motion picture and a TV special.

Eleanor Roosevelt," Mackenzie added. "I hadn't known much about her except that she was a great woman."

One Day at a Time was created by Norman Lear. Lear and his associates have been responsible for many of TV's biggest hits, including *All in the Family, Maude, The Jeffersons,* and *Good Times*.

"When they were casting *One Day at a Time,* they called my manager and asked me to come in," Mackenzie said. "I didn't read for the part. Norman and I just talked. He asked me what I wanted to do, what my problems were, what I thought about kids of divorced parents (Mackenzie and Valerie play the daughters of a divorced woman), and so on." Nothing was definite, but by the end of the meeting, it was clear that Mackenzie had a good chance of getting the part.

"I was so happy and so excited," she exclaimed. "I walked out of Norman's office and down the hall. A water fountain in the hall had been leaking. I fell FLAT. I got wet and I was so embarrassed, but I didn't care. Norman didn't see it, but I told him about it later.

"Norman is a wonderful man. He's like a father. You can go to him with any problem. At first I was frightened of him. He's so important. But the minute I met him, it was like talking to my best friend!"

"Do you find it hard to be in a TV series?" I asked Mackenzie.

"The hardest thing is the schedule," she replied. "One minute you're in school studying art and history, the next minute you're in the studio working on the show. At first my back hurt and my arms hurt, but now it's easy. It flows. We've become a unit. Learning lines isn't hard for me."

When she's not working, Mackenzie attends her regular high school. "After school I take my dog to the park," she said. "I also listen to a lot of music during the day. And I run errands for my aunt. I love to drive. I have a 1976 Pontiac Firebird." She laughed. Her family, she added, also includes "seven crazy cats."

When the show is in production, Mackenzie and Valerie have a tutor on the set. They are required to put in three hours of schooling every day. "We go to school for an hour in the morning," Mackenzie explained. "Then we work until lunchtime. After lunch, we have two more hours of school and then we work until 6:00 p.m. Then I go home and collapse — and watch TV. I watch TV until quite late at night. I like to go to sleep late."

Julie and Barbara try to think up a way to convince their mom that they're old enough to have a party without her being there. Will they succeed?

Mackenzie also likes to go bowling. "One time I made five strikes in a row!" she said proudly.

She likes all kinds of food. "I eat everything!" she said. "I like fettucini, bread, potatoes... I gain weight sometimes, but I just lost five pounds. I'm 5'7" and weigh 110. But I've grown!" She looked horrified and then smiled. "I put on a pair of jeans and they were too short. I'm still growing! My dad is 6'6" and I'm afraid I'm heading up there! Some of my friends used to call me baboon because my arms are so long!"

Mackenzie likes to go to parties. "Not school parties," she explained. "Hollywood parties!" She laughed.

Mackenzie's father is very well known in many circles. I asked Mackenzie how that had affected her life.

"It hasn't really affected my public life," she replied. "He has of course affected my private life. He got me started singing. For a while I felt weird when people would say, 'Mackenzie Phillips, daughter of so-and-so....' Then I decided, 'What's wrong about that? He's my father!' People do it less now, but it doesn't bother me when they do."

Mackenzie loves being recognized by her fans. "Kids stop me a lot and say they see me on the show. I think we're really getting to kids," she said. "They say our stories touch on things they have gone

Sometimes a good heart-to-heart talk is the best way for Julie, Barbara, and their mother to settle day-to-day problems.

through. Valerie and I change our lines sometimes. The writers don't always know kids' lingo. We try to make the scripts as realistic as possible."

It was time for our interview to end. Mackenzie excused herself politely and jumped up. She was going to go looking for a house — for herself, her aunt, her cousin, one dog, and "seven crazy cats."

* * *

Valerie Bertinelli plays Barbara Cooper, Mackenzie's younger sister, on *One Day at a Time*. In real life, she and Mackenzie are almost the same age. Valerie was born April 23, 1960, making her only five months younger than Mackenzie.

"When the show started, I was supposed to be 14," Valerie said. "But after we'd been on the air 13 weeks they made me 15½! My sister is supposed to be 17."

Valerie and I met for luncheon in a flower-filled French restaurant in the San Fernando Valley. Valerie listened intently as the waiter rattled off a long list of French specialties. She asked about one of the chicken dishes, and then ordered that.

Valerie lives in Northridge, California. She was born in Wilmington, Delaware. "We left Delaware when I was eight," she told me. "My father works for General Motors. It's kind of scary to move when you're eight. You have to leave all your friends behind and make a new beginning someplace else. We moved to Michigan. Once we got there, I liked it. We lived near a ski resort. My dad taught me to ski."

Valerie has an older brother and two younger brothers. "We moved as my dad got promoted to better jobs," she explained. "We also moved to Los Angeles, then to Oklahoma, and finally back here to California."

Valerie never thought of being an actress until the family moved to Los Angeles. Then it all came about because she was terribly shy.

Believe it or not, Valerie Bertinelli took up acting because she was too shy! She plays Mackenzie's sensible younger sister, Barbara Cooper, on the show.

"We saw an ad in the newspaper for an acting school," Valerie said. "My father wanted me to try it to get over my shyness. I started taking acting lessons when I was 11. I was scared to death.

"My first audition was for a deodorant commercial," she recalled with a laugh. "My mother took me to the audition. I was so scared! All the girls who were there looked about three years older. I was 12 then."

She didn't get a part in the commercial, but she kept trying. "You have to keep trying," she stressed. "You may go on 100 interviews and not get anything. I always tell myself, 'Well, better luck next time.' A lot of it *is* luck. There are so many talented people around."

Valerie is very close to her family. "They have really kept me going," she said. "They gave me confidence to keep trying."

When she's not working, Valerie is a junior at Granada Hills High School. "I like math and English very much," she said. And I love to play football! I play touch, tackle, flag — everything. I play it in PE (Physical Education), and sometimes people from the studio and I go out on Saturdays and play. My brothers taught me how to play. I'm pretty good!"

Valerie and her co-star Mackenzie Phillips are good friends. Both of them are kept busy with school and work — and they love every minute of it.